# THE LOCAL WORLD

# The Local World

*Poems by*

Mira Rosenthal

The Kent State University Press

*Kent, Ohio*

© 2011 by Mira Rosenthal
Library of Congress Catalog Card Number 2011016823
ISBN 978-1-60635-105-5
Manufactured in the United States of America

The Wick Poetry Series is sponsored by the Stan and Tom Wick Poetry Center and the
Department of English at Kent State University.

LIBRARY OF CONGRESS CATALOGING-IN-PUBLICATION DATA
Rosenthal, Mira.
  The local world : poems / by Mira Rosenthal.
      p.    cm. — (Wick poetry series)
  Includes bibliographical references.
  ISBN 978-1-60635-105-5 (pbk. : alk. paper) ∞
  I. Title.
  PS3618.O8424L63 2011
  811'.6—dc22

                              2011016823

British Library Cataloging-in-Publication data are available.

15  14  13  12  11      5  4  3  2  1

# CONTENTS

# FOREWORD BY MAGGIE ANDERSON

As the editor of the Wick Poetry Series (both the first books and the chapbooks) of the Kent State University Press for more than fifteen years, I have read a great number of first books. I am always attracted to the energy and boldness that characterize a fine new poet's work. I love too the sometimes rough undertones that hint at a voice a bit surprised by its own accomplishment. The very best first books, I think, are those that declare the concerns and projects of a particular moment in time, but that also lay rich groundwork for the poems to come. *The Local World* by Mira Rosenthal is such a book.

*The Local World* includes many poems in which land, the human body, and language come together at a point of both vulnerability and strength. In "Curtain"—perhaps the best poem I have ever read about standing by as helpless witness to the pain of a loved one—the poet is sent away from the hospital room of her wounded sister while the dressing is changed. Though she is compliant, she yearns to stay:

> to at least hear her scream, to hold
> her hand, her head even, while the nurse
> again ripped the bandage off in order
> to keep the wound fresh, keep it fertile
> for grafting.

In another poem, "Salvage and Tarweed," Rosenthal reverses the terms of the metaphor:

> tarweed's taproot
> goes down into land's flesh, deeper
> than turkey mullein or vinegar weed
> or any other native grass, just as language
> goes deeper than skin—which is why
> it survives.

In several poems based on Dorothea Lange's photographs of the evacuation and destruction of California's fertile Berryessa Valley, Rosenthal juxtaposes the narrative of the ruined valley with the narrative of grafting human skin: "*they dug down deep dug down into her body . . . // they dug into her flesh dug into the rotting mess of trauma . . . // they took her tissue living tissue pressed it over the wound like a wet petal.*"

In poem after poem of *The Local World*, the human body and the land are at risk. What mitigates this danger is the power of language to reshape experience. Rosenthal employs multiple levels of diction and image to keep these poems from unrelenting grief, "the minor key," she acknowledges, "of which I am so sedulous a student." In fact, though this poet has difficult stories to tell—"*there are stories forking off there are stories told over and over*"—her central focus throughout is the redemptive power of words. "I *will* say what I mean," Rosenthal writes in "Gentle Art," the first poem in the book. In "Written Image," she declares, "*an image written down becomes the way to build a world ourselves in it /* and I get on."

The central section of *The Local World*, "Necessary Travel," is a group of poems about "being foreign in a foreign country." Here, Rosenthal experiments with form (one-sentence poems, repeated lines, accretion of stanza lengths) in ways that both lighten and deepen the subjects. Happily these poems not only evoke many places ("Bakery, Poland," "Road, India," "Post Office, Slovenia," "Field, Anywhere"), but they also interrogate what travel itself means—"the idea of the place," in Elizabeth Bishop's phrase. These are never mere travelogues but rigorous self-investigations of what it means to wish to be strange or foreign, "to want to glean another's hardship for your vigor, / to want to go and go en route to the interior / further into the foreign in a foreign country."

Inevitably, the poet will have to move on from these foreign places, and in a surprising turn, the last section of the book is in no way a "Dorothy-returns-to-Kansas" ending, but a stunning move into transcendence. The traumatic materials of the earlier poems are still there, but they are now wholly in the service of art. In "Mysticism in the Dark," Rosenthal lists things children are told to allay their fears of the dark and make them brave. She uses here the language of folk tale and dream: "A house is not a house and you are not inside the house. / You are not a body lying in bed / but a bench for something higher to sit down on." In this poem and in others in the last section, I can see how Rosenthal's work as a translator of Polish poetry has informed her own poems. She uses words like a stonemason who knows the way each rock carries soil, water, and the history of everything that has weathered it.

The final poem in *The Local World*, "Sunflower," is longer and more varied in line length and white space than any other in the book. The poet and her sister are together in a garden where a large decayed sunflower must be cut down. The literal work of chopping down the stalk and the metaphorical work the two sisters have to do in order to more safely inhabit their futures, are in perfect balance. The language of each kind of work enriches the other, as in the best poems of Frost:

> The choice a gardener makes, which neck to snap, and we are all
> secondary, all but feeders on sunlight: O, forsaken child . . .

> We must carry this useless body, head and foot, to the compost bin,
> toss it in, give it back.

In a rare use of the exclamatory mode as both anger and wonder, the poet slashes the dead sunflower and lets go of the past:

> what was once said is no longer real: O, never-resting mind . . .
> the past is the past: O, petulant vine . . .
> you can give back.

> And abandon the dead surf of childhood: Say, beauty . . . Your beauty
> . . . O, fine sword . . .

What an eye for the precise detail this poet has, and what wild music! In *The Local World*, Mira Rosenthal has retrieved from a damaged landscape and history a new world of startling wholeness and beauty. It is with the greatest pleasure and admiration that I introduce her to you and welcome her to the table.

# ACKNOWLEDGMENTS

Grateful acknowledgment is made to the editors of the following journals in which some of these poems, sometimes in earlier versions, first appeared:

*The American Poetry Review:* "Curtain," "Mysticism in the Dark"
*Beloit Poetry Journal:* "Heat"
*The Cortland Review:* "Layover," "The Pass"
*Faultline: Journal of Art and Literature: from* "Foreign in a Foreign Country"
*Harpur Palate:* "Estate Sale"
*Notre Dame Review:* "The Matter of the Pears," "Night Latch" (as "4 A.M.")
*Ploughshares:* "Louchébème"
*Seneca Review:* "Sunflower"
*Slate:* "Morphine"
*West Branch:* "Man Leans Forward"

Thanks to the Fulbright Commission for a year outside the United States and normal life that prompted the writing of many of these poems; to the National Endowment for the Arts for a fellowship; and to the MacDowell Colony for a month's stay in which this book took its final form.

My immeasurable thanks for the feedback and encouragement I have received from readers, family, and friends over the years. Thank you in particular to Carol Frost, Maxine Scates, Ross Gay, Eve Grubin, Beth Frost, Sara Harris, and Diana Dunkelberger who read the manuscript at different stages, and to my immediate family for their confidence in my pursuit of poetry. Thank you also to Maggie Anderson—I couldn't have hoped for a more dedicated judge and astute editor—who has kept this series going for over fifteen years. Thank you to Rob and Kassia Zinn for the cover idea. Finally, deep gratitude to my husband, Greg, for his steady love, humor, and collaboration.

# I. Salvage and Tarweed

Digging a hole to where the past is buried,
one covers the living grass on either side.
—*Ellen Bryant Voigt*

# GENTLE ART

the seam ripper between thumb and pointer, you bend your head
　　closer

*like lies like the undoing of lies*

the sewing machine brandishing light

the slight tool with its forked head and blade, as trivial as porcelain,
　　but fierce instead of fragile

*like* no *and* yes *at the same time*

the things your mother teaches you: cook gourmet, sew the blinds,
　　embroider surfaces

the pieces of a pattern cut from see-through tissue paper

the narrative: a third house, a second husband, the step of stepfather

the scissor of psychology he uses to tell you who you are, scrutiny
　　sharp-edged, persuasive

*like pretend like she's saying* pretend *but not speaking*

the analysis a hack of words defining the current design, intractable
　　mind that feels so like false smiling

but you've cut along the wrong line

the selvage scattered round your knees

the number two stitches you can make out now as you pull the join,
　　each loop in the chain

the blade in your hand

*and it will be years you'll take years to find veracity to repeat internally*—I
*will* say what I mean

the tiny tip you slip into the beginning of the seam

the sound of splitting as the metal snaps the sewn thread loose

# WORK

"And then I find myself," my sister says
through the rustle of leaves in the phone,
"still in the orchard, pulling weeds."
And I know what she means—where I am,
traveling again, down on the short carpet
leaning against the hotel's mini fridge,
receiver pulled tight to reach; where she is
crouching somewhere cleaning a barn's stall
all weekend at a Gurdjieff work retreat;
and where we go in memory, Gravenstein
apple, Clingstone peach, Bosch pear,
the base of each trunk painted white
to slick the surface against ants that attract
the swallows that start the process of decay.
We worked in the field every Saturday
where incarnadine soil was set with clay.
"Just try," our stepfather would say.
"Just try to pick up the shovel. You do
or you don't. There's no such thing as trying."
So we learned to be self-help junkies,
a forever replenished serving of moods.
Now my sister's explaining her spiritual fast,
that she's watching her mind holding on
to anger, looking for emotion like an ant
for traction up the branch to the peach
to pierce its blushing skin, begin the wound.
"Excruciating," she says of our family fictions,
as if there is sap in her veins, slowing
her heart down.
                    Half our lives since then.
To say excruciating is an exaggeration.
It was a Babcock peach with fluorescent flesh
and a ribbed pit you could pry open to find
its bitter almond. And when we rose, we left
two depressions in the soil. And weeds left

deep creases on the flat caps of our knees,
texture to trace with the sensitive tip of a finger
till those hard indentations released.

# CURTAIN

My sister asked me to go out into the hall.
I went out into the hall. She asked me
to go farther, not just down the hall
but to the other side of the trauma ward
where the bank of windows faced west
and where, during the third dressing change,
I sat in the chair by the elevator and tried
to persuade myself that the setting sun
felt good on my skin, was warming me.
But really I was plotting how to cheat,
to sneak back on her side of the hospital,
not only on her side but next to her door,
not only next to but inside the door,
to be inside and with her when the nurse
drew the gray curtains, when the flowers
on the sill were trapped between window
and cloth, pressed up against the glass
like some embalmed specimen. I felt
the same crease of cool air slicing her
in half, turning over onto her stomach,
the thin gown sliding open in back,
the spine, the cleaving calves, we are
two halves. And I watched the nurse
placing white gauze in a stack, counted
the morphine drips, tried to find some sort
of rhythm in it all, some sort of pattern,
the way her skin would later be, meshed
by making lengthwise nicks in succession,
stippled like the pincushion of a seamstress
who kept her needles meticulous in rows
down and across in the cushion's flesh.
And all of this to be torn apart. Yes,
to at least hear her scream, to hold
her hand, her head even, while the nurse
again ripped the bandage off in order

to keep the wound fresh, keep it fertile
for grafting. But she had asked me
to go out into the hall. I sat in the chair
on the west side of the building and
pretended to find patience in warmth
while she screamed over there, screamed
because there was nothing left to try,
no anodyne that would be strong enough.
And she asked me to go into the hall.
And she screamed because it was wrong
and she wouldn't say that it was wrong
and she wouldn't let me see so that I
might say that it was wrong. I sat there
with only my careless imagination, a mirror
unable to reflect from such a distance
without distorting, a lung inhaling smoke,
that it may be closer to numbness and pain.

# MORPHINE

The window to this world opened again
as the drips slowed, and she became
whippy as a sheet of glass improperly
annealed, ready to smash at any
indefinite touch in a whining matrix
of stresses, the bed frame a museum box
where she lay, encased as a mummified
kestrel tailed with a fleece of fetid cloth
laid out by the mongoose (pharaoh's rat)
cradled in the nook of a dead arm,
and her eyes were intensified as soup
with beef bouillon and parsnip, potato,
celery ends, the candor of bread and butter
to swallow the fact of what happened.

PHOTOGRAPH: WESTWARD

the state will have to pay for this

*they dug down deep dug down into her body*

the photograph we're looking at could be a scene from Anasazi ruins,
centuries past now outlined center beams of stone and holes for
where the living once had lived

the flooding will commence in three weeks' time, the caption says

the fertile valley now forgone to reservoir, cisternal

*they dug into her flesh dug into the rotting mess of trauma*

the uniformed and sanctioned men came into Berryessa Valley,
disintered the caskets, carried them down the road—headstones
and all—on their shoulders

the family plot: autologous, a derivation, the marrow within our bones

the camera's flash bleaches California's orange poppies colorless and
skeletal in the photograph before

and after?

*they took her tissue living tissue pressed it over the wound like a wet petal*

the higher ground the men prepared ahead of time, identical plots
where they'd bury those same old bodies

and what's the point of that, my sister asks, why not head farther west
to the middle of the sea, where there is no worry of earthquakes?

*she took the bullet took it straight on the calf and afterward an epicenter
a dead center where her being once had been*

the middle of the sea, she says, where we'll walk on water, plow the waves,
raise cattle on sea foam

the likelihood: who knows, maybe we'll even strike gold

# THE MATTER OF THE PEARS

When I said the seven pear trees,
the ones I had just shown her,
when we had just walked beneath
their branches going dormant
at summer's end, a few leaves
flagging the orchard's bearing
where we circled, looking
for last berries of the season
where stubborn vines persisted,
but we were late and there were none,
so we sat on the grass by the stump
of the evergreen that died last year,
that used to hold a swing
where we twisted and untwisted
till we were high when we were young . . .

When I said the seven pear trees
give us so much new fruit,
we don't know what to make
with bins of pears that rot
and you know when one goes,
the tendency to ferment
catches the others' flesh
like fire, like flames consuming
succulence, before you can preserve
brandied pears or pear butter,
the whole batch is gone,
and she sat there leaning forward,
listening and smoking
like she already knew the eager
fleeting nature of flavor.

And it was simply about the seasons
when I said the seven pear trees
give us so much new fruit

that we fail to cull the essence
before it goes to mold,
and it was a simple metaphor
when I said flesh catches
like wood catches fire—
before you can act, you're gone—
and she leaned back like a smoldering log
thick enough to withstand the smoke,
then, "Just like vice," she said,
and I was nervous and jealous,
wishing I had thought of that
when speaking of the trees.

# PHOTOGRAPH: MAN LEANS FORWARD

it's been like this for weeks now, like I'm stuck in a photo titled *Untitled*

*a watch as in the periods of ancient night as in more than one darkness*
*divides me*

it's the one where a middle-aged man sits in his general store, OPEN
sign behind him in the window, boy biking by with his dog trailing

it's black and white, of course, of a time when one could put in such
orders as "give me a can of brake fluid and a package of Wheaties"

*a watch as in Hamlet falling into sadness then into a fast and thence to*
*a watch*

it's the way the man leans forward, elbows on his bended knees, in
hand an open newspaper

it's his hands, well inked, articulated

it's his multiple roles as postmaster and free farm advisor and crop
insurance salesman for those who come through the door

it's a swarm of rubber bands balled in a drawer behind him

*a watch as in a flock of birds a watch of nightingales like how we end up*
*gathering nuance twisting into ourselves*

it's the door, which might as well be stenciled with the words *as my*
*father did before me* instead of the name *McKenzie's*

it's because his father is part of this

it's the way everything that passes through our hands becomes an axis
around which we turn, a tether

*a watch as in the art of falconry a keeping of the hawk from sleep in order to tame it a conquering of lineage through falling into line*

it's why he doesn't look straight at us but aims his gaze beyond the open shutter

it's the shutter, opening

# NIGHT LATCH

Maybe it's only heartburn, this feeling
that my skin is taut against a knife
I have swallowed whole. It pierces,
and everything else in the darkened room—
my hand held up in front of my face,
the lightning sketching ribs inside
the blinds, the trace of lacy drapes—
is nothing compared to such a sting.
It pierces, and fine white petals
budding on the plum tree out the window
are streaming from branches in the storm
the way I imagine skin detaches from
the carcass of a cow in the Ganges River
because I've heard they throw the holy in
full-bodied without having cremated them:
the babies, the devout old men, and cows.
Maybe I should travel to see that river,
forms floating, bold and skeletal, go
beyond the saying *getting my day started,*
because a saying does not consider
the stick causing a riptide in the current
of one day to the next, or how starting
never ends. The widowed arrive from
all over the country to pass time watching
the sacred pyres. The dying are everywhere
waiting, haunting the pathways, year upon
year, in their white gauze of mourning,
shrouded like me under this white sheet.
But they aren't dead, not yet. An acute point
of pain from which everything radiates.
And their wish to be buried in a holy place
is simply a waste of life, the beginning,
the ending. Why not start from the middle:
*This is a knife, a knife inside my chest. I will live
by cutting myself out from the inside.*

# POWERLESS FLIGHT

A pebble is floating at eye level in the air.
You think I'm only saying this to grab
your attention and hear myself speak.
But the pebble is floating off the floor
of a cockpit carrying two seated passengers,
one a mother and the other, of course, me.
Past the little dot hovering, see the mother,
no longer flesh pressed in a belt but some
euphoric substance, if only briefly. It's the half-
second just after the towplane cuts the aircraft
loose to glide on the thermal updraft
that hits the cliff and rises at the top.
The two bodies rise off their cushions,
suspended loosely in their same old clothing.
And the mother—poet, imp her wing on words
or at the very least on momentary stasis—
is smiling at the tickle of her drifting earrings,
at weightlessness. Then the glider swings out
over the city park where her husband waits,
over the valley and its neat rows of grape
as wind sings in the cabin and mountains
train the eye into the distance. Now the pebble
is gone from the air, and the mother too,
and, believe me, the poet who might repair
the theory of herself: what the mind keeps
chasing in the silence we held above.
Only gravity remains, and the repeating
release of a pebble dropping to the floor,
and the texture of wind leaking into space.

# WRITTEN IMAGE

a streetcar in my mind

a woman driving the streetcar, blue serge suit, money changer slung
round her waist

*an agency as thick as wool as pathos*

a pointing with her thumb, an urging, a charge this character possesses

a focus: she never takes no, never stops or goes home, never waits to
enact what she means

*an agency as deep as echo as bright as mirrored flame*

and orange traffic cones repeat in each of the streetcar's celestory
windows

a forest of buildings empties into night

and the smell of wet concrete applies itself to skin, a salve for the long
day, a strong talc

*they say we have no agency they say we're only acted on hypothesized
postmodern*

a watchman from his marbled lobby watches the loop car approaching

a glow whites his cheek, his cap collecting and repooling lamplight

a book in his hands

*an image written down becomes the way to build a world ourselves in it*

and I get on

# SALVAGE AND TARWEED

I know a little what it's like to leave
a place. The year is 1990, I am sixteen,
and there are sounds of ripping wood
for salvage, the buzz of insects, the sharp
citrus smell of yellow tarweed in the air,
as it has always been. Long after most
things splinter and split in this dryness,
tarweed survives, exuding a sticky substance
on the surface of its leaves, coating the cow's
muzzle, darkening the horse's fine lashes
like mascara. My stepfather is dismantling
planks of a water drum disintegrating
in California sun. How many masks have I
tried on to deal with his verbal razing?
Better that he drank, used alcohol as solvent
for ruinous resin, better that the effects
of his psychoanalyzing were visible cracks
on the surface of my face I could talk about
when you ask. But tarweed's taproot
goes down into land's flesh, deeper
than turkey mullein or vinegar weed
or any other native grass, just as language
goes deeper than skin—which is why
it survives. If this valley were chosen
to be dammed, as Berryessa was in 1957,
I'd document it in pictures like Lange,
soak photographic paper in thick emulsion,
see it all in nostalgic black and white.
There'd still be time to bring the cattle
down from the hills, time for a few homes
to be reassembled on higher ground,
before orderly demolition began. But
my stepfather isn't going to be moved,
not for any flood, not for hydroelectric
development called progress, not for me.

I've come to say goodbye, he takes his glove
off, fumbles in his pocket. "Good luck," he says,
pressing a twenty in my hand. Field of yellow
viscid blooms blur behind him in swales,
as it has always been, I take my leave.

## II. Necessary Travel

There are times when we *want* to be aliens and strangers, to feel how the shape of our lives is not the only shape, to drift before a catalog of possible lives . . .
—*Lewis Hyde*

I was born lost and take no pleasure in being found.
—*John Steinbeck*

# LOUCHÉBÈME

a man sitting across from me in a French restaurant in New York City

*a name is a word is the first form of domestication*

an explanation of the secret language he spoke with his father in the
    marketplace in *la Villette: lincsé* for five francs, *larante* for forty and the
    word for money, *le leurrebem,* meaning *butter*

a son's desire to name the world for himself

a play of sound: jargon, argot, slang invented in the meat shops in Paris

a leaning in, a gesticulation

*a butcher some butter the dealing and purchase the price is in secret*

an accent that grows thick like churned milk

*a buffalo eye hung with light hung with death a kind of rapture*

a stall with a hardwood cutting block oiled so the indentations feel
    smooth to the palm

a shaft of sunlight slanting from a window, a glint whenever the blade
    passes through

a halo of dust, a solitary moment, a father leaning over into light

*a hand resting mid-slice resting in thought a kind of rapture*

a cutting block knife, a customer standing on the other side of the counter

*that woman shifting from foot to foot she doesn't know what I'm saying
    to my son a language becomes a body that outlasts us we are in the
    final account silent*

a fact: he talks of money and meat without the woman knowing his
  dealing, without her knowing the knives

a quick volley of words that fly from the pocket of his mouth to carve
  for me his memory

a restaurant in New York City, a recollection of not flesh but language

a recollection of a workbench, some light, what came before America,
  before he had any accent at all

# LAYOVER

A boy, about nine, is flinging the tethered
ball of each of his fists successively
in the space between us sitting opposite,
only to him we're not in an airport.
He's boxing some invisible opponent
in the air in a ring that's materialized
around him, leathery ropes springing
with the force of what he's naming: *left jab,*
*right hook.* His eyelids droop, forehead
tipped forward, eyes two taut mitts.
His knuckles flick in tight formation,
five, then more too quick to call,
as his toes continue their rhythmic bounce
on the arena floor of the stained carpet.
I fake reading, pretend not to notice
as the made-up fist of the boy's opponent
clocks his jaw, and a ripple takes the surface
of his face. His head flips back so hard
it skips against the plastic chair, goes calm.
*One, two, three . . .* he begins to count.
And I, like a spectator, safe in the crowd
of my book, feel myself counting with him,
just as we've all been counting inches of snow
since morning, waiting for the sky to break
light, to find we're once again home.
Once I returned from a trip to discover
the faint music of wings playing against
the wall: a bird caught in the chimney
and no way to get it out. It kept knocking
the mortar concealing it, fraying, I pictured,
the tip of each oiled feather, crumbling
bit by bit the inner structure of the flue,
lost to itself and the light, lodged deep
in the soot of the house. And that moment
comes back in this, the boy, myself

watching him play at fighting, revive
deep in the count, which is what keeps me
mesmerized, inadvertently gazing. The boy
reaches up, pulls the lip of his knit cap down
over his face, clips the tension to the tip
of his chin. And then he's simply in it,
head sheathed, imagination flickering
in the dark, on the wooly scrim.

# OKEFENOKEE

It was Sunday and nothing was concluded.
The boardwalk planks thunked against
their stilts as we passed and every stick
was the ridged back of an alligator
in our consciousness slicing the surface
of the swamp, which stretched two tendrils
of water so dark and still into the foliage
that forests of trunks and dangling moss
grew backward into its parallel depths,
fermenting leaves the only smell
of what was once land now dredged
for miles into muck and lilies to get lost in,
dampness so pervasive that the fire
of one's life on shore couldn't hiss
its way through, lay smoldering, unseen
in the slow-moving shadow below
our canoe. And the paddle was a stent
in the heart of water, draining all reflection.

THE BORDER

a room partitioned by Formica countertop and glass

a woman at a desk, her nose bobbing, placing checks in columns
inexorably

*what does it mean to pass to fit behind a face?*

a see-through pane of glass that's made all wall and then all window by
shifting light

a line of worn-out people waiting for a status

a way of plainly maintaining sanity: forms approved, biography that's
spoken for

*what does it mean to be of a mind to find your thoughts are specious?*

an arbitrary edge, a being on edge

a homeless man who can't stand still but tries to keep his place in line
while prancing like a tap dancer, shoes all cracked and black with
grime

an urge to have a turn

*what does it mean to be checked off to pass the threshold of repletion?*

an urge for a turn at the counter, a quiet *ma'am, may I?*

a tensing of all joints to hold his agitated state of mind, become a
soldier at the window, or maybe more a boy at attention, ready for
his merit badge, prize for first place

an urge to say you're here, complete, a being on the verge

*what does it mean to cross to be received to reach the sanctum of the tenable?*

a stance the man's feet cannot keep

a sudden seizure of tapping stirring his legs, possessing his hips, a
  rhythmic beat against the wall dividing here from there

a glance of understanding the woman gives the man

a little crack in the glassed-in panel that separates us from them, a
  space where her arm uncoils to place an apple in his hand

*what does it mean to see the self in contrast to attract one's inverse
  madness to alleviate a lack?*

an act of witness, how the man takes up a march back down the line,
  salutes each one of us in turn still waiting patiently

an inexorable ceremony of charity

a limit in each one of us that makes us look away

# FOREIGN IN A FOREIGN COUNTRY

You arrive at night and deplane on the tarmac,
feeling as all new travelers must, your language
orphaned in the palm fronds, useless in the airport
where the guards issue blank stares and laugh,
and you ride in the back of a pickup with baggage
to a mountain town where they ration comforts
three hours each morning, and water drums
populate yards, and roads are bone-dry clay,
and now those who live here stand about
and watch chickens flap to the rusty rims
and peck out the eye of the sun that sways
there, multiplying its orb, its bands of light
on each shiny surface, a schematic glare
to guide by on the other side of the equator
where you are foreign in a foreign country.

## 2. ROOM, ANYWHERE

Then there is jet lag, that wooden joint
sliding in and out of its socket moaning
against the inverse of time, and you
in the dark with your eyes for sight,
but there is only wall and corner undimming
from which you can't construct a finite room,
where you are, where you are breathing into,
breathing out of and all you want is the clear
persistent sound air makes in the groove
of the throat—sleep soundly—keep to
one body and soul set in this, not that other
place you fear to name or you will cave
in to nostalgia, capitulate to the person
you used to be, but now you can be anyone,
start from being foreign in a foreign country.

## 3. ROAD, INDIA

Because here the scorpion clings to the dark
and you have to tap each empty boot
against the floor and turn the heel to verify
the void, and because its body seems prehistoric
and pocket-size, when you come upon one out
on the road in broad daylight, you have to try,
and so you circle it for an arc,
raise the point of your umbrella and poke
and prod its obverse underside
until the coals of self-protection spark,
such a sting as when you try to put
yourself into the epic, but history multiplies
your little life away, and then the glow
loses its intensity and is again a curio,
simply something foreign in a foreign country.

## 4. TRAIN CAR, HUNGARY

You end up watching rather than speaking
to strangers in the train car, one with the look
of a banker, one with a tattoo of an anchor
bobbing on his bulbous forearm, as if his flexing
was meant to free it from the bedrock
of experience, which tends to lighten the picture,
fade the ink of past conviction—
you fall to finding company in the silent,
facing he who's facing backward, the sense
he's looking back on life too soon
already at forty, opening the fist, closing it,
a semaphore in the anchor's oscillations
that signals resignation, and you're drawn
into acceptance, to that kind of calm,
giving in to the foreign in a foreign country.

## 5. BAKERY, POLAND

A window, and beyond a hemlock hedge
thronged with sky between the flowers,
the land turned mud by rain's tantrum—
is this the town your great-grandmother fled?—
then the sudden hum of many sparrows
rustling in the deadly *Conium maculatum,*
two-times-twelve-times-twenty-four pinions—
more years than you can trace your background back—
and your tongue is silent as a frog under water,
the town's name unpronounceable, legions
of bees uncountable behind the baker's rack,
their labor turning levulose—this is second nature,
to want to glean another's hardship for your vigor,
to want to go and go en route to the interior
farther into the foreign in a foreign country.

## 6. POST OFFICE, SLOVENIA

Though you live in a room with bare walls,
sleep on a bed without sheets, the cold walk
to the neighborhood post office (letter sent daily)
keeps you from becoming misplaced material:
you are not the stray cork a seagull tries to choke
down in one piece, not the river haunting clay
beneath your feet where you follow the path
of its old course, diverted, not the plastic
bag that flaps in the branches of the chestnut
like some expressionist splash on an abstract
canvas, art for art's sake, and you think
each piece is fragment, but beautifully put,
and you would, if possible, cast an absentee
ballot for everything lost, yet closer to you
than your own leg walking in a foreign country.

The horizon, you see, from your vantage
on a park bench at dusk in a random city,
turns the large and the small alike into a tree,
makes the turrets of the castle look like foliage,
takes a little animated man and his quirky
tilt of the head, as if he were a pigeon in the scree,
and his hop-skip every third step to keep pace,
and stills him till he fades into the rest, far off,
out there, and you know, from this leveling
of all forms to a forest in the distance,
from this purposeful dislocation of a self,
that the unspoken search which keeps you traveling
is for that moment before perspective sets in, a sense
of Lilliputian strings, your own relevance
distinct against the forest in a foreign country.

## 8. MARKET, INDIA

And then you find it here, the Main Street
of your home, the circadian rhythm of a town,
a vendor slack bodied at his stand of goods
on the corner, a hundred brands of cigarettes
and magazines, and ice cream in the window
of a child's eye, and pausing, hereabouts—
along with the purse hawker yelling his price
like an auctioneer, a mantra chanted fast enough
to lose meaning, along with the flick of a wrist
counting out some change, that deft nuance
of skill grasped through repetition, aloof—
for a moment void of the capacity to quest
after something else, you forget the difference,
and your old life comes back with force
inside of you, foreign in a foreign country.

## 9. FIELD, ANYWHERE

So: you want to live the way only a great body
of all the same thing ceaselessly keeps turning
back into itself, like the wind, like the ocean,
to wander into the tough blades on the sunny
hill and feel the sting of the cut and keep going,
where the trampled stalks smart the eye with onion,
till you are aware of a new sharpness
welled up inside and feel once more
that desire to return to the local world
and belong, like an oak barrel after the process
of wine making, with both the acrid and sugar,
to linger like light, like smells that bring to mind
many fields and suggest not play, exactly,
but that same absorption and oblivious joy
of being foreign in a foreign country.

# HEAT

A languor sitting down on the stone lap of Buddha.
In Rishikesh the heat was foretold and exact.

The chanting of *bhajans* infusing the town
as I was walking by the languor sitting like Buddha.
In Rishikesh the heat was foretold and exact.

Sweat cooled by the breeze off the Ganges River.
Wind carrying *bhajans* through the dress of soft cotton
covering me as I walked by the monkey and the statue.
In Rishikesh the heat was foretold and exact.

Concentration required for a simple silence. Smell of *samosas*
browning in grease. Sweat of the body's boiling and motion.
The breeze off the *Ganga,* the chanting of *bhajans*
infusing my walking and the languor sitting on Buddha.
In Rishikesh the heat was foretold and exact.

Green saplings over the hill where the water falls. Thoughts drifting
through the mind in concentration, in a simple silence,
when the smell of hot batter frying in oil descended
into evening, into prayer, into *bhajans.* The rustle
of my walking startled the monkey who sat cross-legged
with Buddha. A red sun in Rishikesh, heat foretold and exact.

The smell of diesel from rickshaws careening down the hill
where boys soaked in hot water, thinking nothing, thinking simply
about frying *samosas,* flies buzzing beyond them,
and *sadhus* sat cross-legged singing and chanting
as I passed and the sun bit the lip of the river, sank light
into stone of a statue, into hair, into silver on the back of a monkey
running from Buddha. A red sun in Rishikesh, heat foretold, exact.

# THE PASS

At this point turning back will take longer than moving forward.
The Langtang Valley slips into the trees. Already we
have climbed beyond ideas of exhaustion.

A dirt path narrows to ten small steps.
We take the stairs.
Then even the crude ends—a gash of what was stone
brought down to dust. A landslide.

The path snakes through pale rubble.
A faint line like an animal track through grass
hinting upward. I stop and look down the long run.

Boulders have been put to bed
in their own quick chips, under a dusty blanket,
settled in an even line
over sapling, fern, any green once clinging
to the mountain now covered
in a rush. Ahead, a hiker's red shirt flames and waves
as it bobs away—I sway,

am swaying—in me a magnet drawn
to the valley's core, to the river's channel.
I cannot move from the bare site, on the edge
of this moment the body resists and invites.

All the water in me wants to plunge to earth.

# III. Mysticism in the Dark

I have to blind myself artificially in order to focus
all the light on one dark spot.
  —*Sigmund Freud*

As children we were warned not to whistle at night for fear of evil spirits.
Dangerous animals became even more
sinister and uncanny in the dark.
A snake was never called by its name at night because it would hear.
It was called a string.
A beetle the size of a child's fist was never pointed out to have pinchers.
It was called a button.
A spider in the web of its life didn't have poison secreted away
nor the sticky means with which to entrap.
It was purely called an apple hanging on a branch.
A black bat wasn't fast enough to swoop into anyone's hair, get tangled
    there.
It was called a paper snowflake.
It was called a falling leaf.
A lizard bent around a branch
was a headband you wear to keep hair out of your face.
A cricket was simply a clothespin.

The bigger animals were nothing more than clothing tossed out.
A bear was a worn-through winter jacket.
A fox, a scarf rubbed down to beaded threads.
And that praying mantis stuck up against the wall,
only a necklace to adorn your thin collarbones.
A scorpion is merely the bent latch from a window.
A silverfish is just a drop of coffee.
Two cockroaches paused on cement,
plainly a pair of sunglasses dropped and forgotten in the hustle of the day.
A line of ants, straight stitches on the hem of the tablecloth
at which you'll sit in the morning.

And what is that roll of toilet paper doing
hooting from the ridge of the roof?
And why is the lamp shade creeping stealthily through the courtyard
and hopping up on the rim of the open garbage can?
And how is that small water bottle inching slowly forward,

leaving its saliva, a trail of where it has been
pointing to where it is going?
And who scattered those twenty plump babies' shoes under the bush
and what makes them chirp and dance around
like popcorn in the fryer?
They seem to be looking for something so small
they can't find it, pecking as they are with their blunt toes.
A house is not a house and you are not inside the house.
You are not a body lying in bed
but a bench for something higher to sit down on.
If only you could move your wooden legs and stand up,
everything would be revealed in an instant.

# SNAPSHOTS OF THE FARM BEFORE WE SOLD

\*

Mistletoe all through the oak,
rubbery prehistoric in the crux
of its host—how much will it cost us
this year?—suckers spreading.

\*

Bonfire fed with the brine
of stealthy-rooted blackberry vine—
is that blue juice at the heart
of the flame?—ashy
spoils puddled after ongoing
battle with weedy abundance.

\*

Side field we worked to clear
all summer, hacking away at the pack
of leaves—olly olly oxen free!—
our four cats roaming
out there with the spirits
of what we once had.

\*

What we once had: pigs, goats, trampoline, sheep,
pits in the gravel road, old evergreen tree
with a swing, and rain, rain, rain—will it
ever stop?—gushing from wooly
bodies we evacuate
to higher ground.

\*

Fermenting red button pyracantha
berries the birds wash down—what
was that?—flying headlong drunk
into the floor-to-ceiling
glass, cracked pane.

\*

Unlucky trunk with a vee that once
began to split down the middle,

so we drilled holes, inserted bolts
with nuts to hold the cable taut
but flexible enough—are those the basics
of psychology?—to bind opposing halves
but bend when storm blows through the boughs.

    *

Tree guy going
higher and higher all
pulleys and levers, his saw
ready to hack off the base
of those suckers—what simple
essential machinery—he
hoists into the leaves.

    *

Rotting fence posts wicking water up
the vein of dead wood grain, growing
beer bellies of moisture, toupees
of fresh moss—I guess this is
goodbye old men—we're
selling, we're moving to town.

and we take the rise hiking Clifty Falls in Indiana, the first on the path
    in the morning heat

*there are stories forking off there are stories told over and over*

and inchworm threads thread our eyelids and noses and mouths we keep
    grasping at

and invisible binding binds us, makes our bodies trussery, with sweat
    and sticky web collecting forearm, shoulder, chest

*there are stories stuck there are stories that hold like duct tape*

and then we go down

and occasional gusts toss black and yellow caterpillars into underbrush,
    a flat boulder to sit on, some bread and cheese to eat

and we watch the stream twist off toward working smokestacks and
    the Ohio

and there's a sound of industry: a distant motor underneath it all, the
    minor key of which I am so sedulous a student

and you say: what was it again?

*there are questions there are stories about unfair questions that stick in
    your hair like gum*

and you say: what was it about pain?

and I tell it, how my stepfather would use psychology to keep us going,
    hiking California's Yolla Bolly Wilderness, straps pinching flesh

and he would ask: where do you *go* with your pain?—our bodies sore and
blistered, our sore minds blistering

and he would sit us there, and analyze, and say: I know what your
neurosis is, but I'm not going to tell you

*there are stories swallowed stories like capsule pills the slow release kind*

where *does* our pain go?

these miles and miles in, the heavy pack I take off, the craggy exposed
roots on the way to water

and I stumble, without accustomed weight, a lightness that felt even
then like floating into ether

# CHORE

Sunday chore, small piece, piece of time, time-consuming need, need to
steal away, away from turning around again, again coercion of the mind to
analyze and describe, describe a miniature China plate with yellow design
and gilded edge, edge of a stapler my stepfather threw against the wall so
hard it unhinged, unhinged wooden stand the plate fit in, in the story the
next day in place of anger he gives me the plate, plate of sorrow and sorry
and all the right words he doesn't say, says instead *for your own good* and
*earn your keep*, I keep the plate on a special shelf in my room, room after
room my task is to wipe clean, clean as a business transaction with a maid
hired for wage, wage verbal war and then resort to a stapler, stapler with
heft like the old-fashioned kind, kind words accumulating and unused
after, after chores are done you can go out of your mind, mind like a shelf,
shelf of cheap trinkets, trinkets I still dust every Sunday.

# HOUSEHOLD OBJECTS

when the former tenants left a metal desk they couldn't lift, left inside the
house, in what was once a child's room

*now is a moment and a moment is porous frame*

when the grass grew long enough to check the toolshed for a blade

when the desk got in the way

when we found some space inside the shed, found two old mowers,
both with motors, both emitting an elixir of gasoline

*now is a correlative is an alternative implied*

when we needed elbow room: sufficient latitude to dwell in slippage,
dwell outside the story of our lives

when we slid the metal-framed colossus through the house on
cardboard across linoleum, carpet, floorboard

when the desk reached grassy yard and one leg sunk in filler dirt

when we had to flip it end to end, a thunderous tumble reverberating
metallic echo

*now is a movement is a thing displaced is the trace of a dinosaur sticker
floating on a child's bedroom wall*

when we jockeyed the desk into the shed, opposite the leaky corner,
under the shelf with broken baskets, pots, and potting soil

when we shut the door

*now the wooden latch is chewed away some natural force is chewing you
have to prop a two-by-four against the door to keep it closed in wind
and rain the pebbles pelt it*

when, a calm night on the back porch lit with kerosene, we could smell
    from there the panacea of gasoline, recall the metal monster, shed
    some light on change

when we stood there like pressboard, rain-ingested glue and sawdust of
    discarded selves                            .

# MAN IN WINDOW

> it is human nature to stand in the middle of a thing
> —*Marianne Moore*

There's a still point for him too, standing
by the window in the living room where I can
see him at dusk, outlined by a TV flashing blue
he's no longer watching, instead standing
near the kitchen door, gazing at her by the sink
cleaning dishes, placing each plate, bowl, glass,
and the leveling sound of water falling
that commanded him to get up,
that reminds him of what? The fall
of her hair and the curling current
at the nape of her neck where he's now
swimming, out and then back doing laps
along her shoulder blade like that rhythmic
static of a needle in the middle of a record
played to its end. Yes, a still point, the thought
that any moment she might turn her head
and find him standing there, discovered
alone by himself, that he might turn
and find me in his yard, staring. It is the same
compulsion as when he gets up at night
and on his way to the bathroom, stops
at the washing machine still on and lifts
the lid. A column twisting cloth and water, water
and cloth, gray detergent writing foreign signs
like oil spilled on the page of the sea.
And he's looking in to see what? Water
and cloth, but also the muscle of its rhythm,
the rhythm that's compelling his life, their life
together, dinner and dish, dinner and dish . . .
And we're trying to decide, as he stands there
in the window, as I stand there on his lawn,

if here is a picture of love, or if there's something
more constant, unseen, a motor, a motion,
churning the simple milk of life to the butter
churned milk and salt eventually become.

ESTATE SALE

A yellow sign tacked to a stick of wood
points traffic down Sacramento Street
and leads here, a middle-class neighborhood:
square patches of lawn, small lots, closed shutters,
sometimes a driveway of new laid concrete.
At the house of the deceased, red stone stairs
lead up to the door and you can walk right in
past a fat man smiling from his seat
at a table, money box before him.
"Through the kitchen you'll find the den downstairs,"
all smiles and eagerness and conceit.
"And more out the back. Also upstairs."
By the sink every cupboard stands bare
for want of dishes, now tables replete
with stacks of plates, glasses, and silverware.
At an open drawer, a young woman stands,
head bent, hair brown with one gray streak
hanging forward as she inspects the brand
on a silver serving spoon. "How 'bout this?
Is this one antique?" Her friend dismisses it
and she looks again, not wanting to miss
anything. A stairwell leads to the den—
dark, quiet, no one milling about,
a paneled bar and blackness at one end,
at the other a door that leads outside.
Between here and there, two male voices meet
in conversation, as if meant to chide:
"A shame, a real shame"—their words bear
knowledge that feeds on absence, burns through it—
"I was her caretaker for fifteen years."
And within what sounds like a script, just
what you would expect to hear, a receipt
for the deceased, these voices, whirling, hushed,
there's the tenor of hovering tragedy.
Maybe she's still here, trying to retreat

but unable, so soon, to fade away.
In the bathroom, a woman at the sink
inspects a bottle of aspirin, the sleek
pills in her palm each perfect and distinct.
She keeps it, as if a common bottle
held renewal for the living, a unique
blessing to take from a house she will
only step into once. In the tangle
of polyester clothes on the bed sheet
there's a loose crocheted vest of gray wool.
It's handmade, and by the chair a canvas
bag spills full of yarn. You've found her seat.
If you were to sit down here in her place
would your back ache immediately, ache
and begin to radiate a dull heat
as if the chair were a back-breaking stake
to mark the dead in her ground? If you stay,
her life wrapped around you in the quiet,
will you feel her hand on your shoulder: *stay?*

# PHOTOGRAPH: ANTEDILUVIANS

*We're going to have to scatter out,* someone says.
Someone else opens an orange in silence.
They've stacked the boxes by the door
and out the window two figures walk
away through a field of tarweed along ruts
where truck tires have pulled up grass
and written two parallel lines in the dirt
that last into the distance. Both elderly,
both wearing hats, the woman cradling
a flute of brown paper wrapped around
what looks like some sort of bouquet,
taking flowers while they're walking through
fields of them. All of it a part of them
dissipating like the fine scent and mist
of orange that leaves behind a residue
on the palm that dries to greenish stickiness
they'd probably wait a while to wash off.
Or like an old-fashioned accent lingering
at the neck. *Perhaps,* murmurs the photograph
in musty black and white, *Perhaps there are
moments of peace, complex, intuitive, foretold,
when one purveys what once had been, as if
skimming an old map, and feels worldly.*
The room is empty, save two abandoned
portraits left on the floor on purpose,
black torsos clad in cassocks topped
with striking framed faces, as if the oval
of a captured countenance could scare away
the ghostly crow who will come to pick
at the matter of absence. Out of remnants,
what can be preserved? Nothing, idea at best.
And so, we take with us only flowers
that will never outlast, endure, survive.

## PANIC ATTACK

We're in the kitchen when my sister feels
the house get up, lift itself up on its mortar
legs, turned somehow mortal, and start walking
toward the sea. She doesn't explain the build
of ingredients for the galette she's making
or how the sea enters breath to drown her.
And I can't see when the house's rhythmic gait
sends books and pages fluttering dim reason
down the hardwood hall, black-and-white
pictures in frames on the south wall lilting
like iridescent gills breathing in a wash of waves.
The scene of the disaster down by the dock
inundates the room, the tide of protest and
police and rubber bullets shot directly against
the crowd. She keeps her back to me and I
go on spooning strawberry jam as spilled
detergent rubs tiles raw, the mirror now
in shards, wires coming loose like exposed
veins. The hematoma grows to such a size
they have to saw it out, graft skin like plaster
over the hole. She hears glasses fly from cupboards,
plates pile themselves out on the floor, fists
of canned goods beating the closed door.
But she tries to hide the rise of hyperventilating,
standing there, hands in the dough, gluten
forming threads she pulls, tying knots, till taking
one breath is like heaving the constructed world,
house upon house, by a single tender filament
with the muscle of her only human lungs.

# SUNFLOWER

*For Willow*

What else can you do when a plant has rotted into its own stalk: O, . . .

What else can you do when ants feed after what has decayed: O, the day . . .

thriving on the minerals of death.
The sunflower's old head drooping
where we stood in the middle of the garden.
A plot

> filled with rubble, slabs of cracked foundation, blackberry vines,
> underground
> creepers, taken over
> the back lot: O, roots . . .

You cleared it all, brought in fresh earth, tested for lead: O, façade . . .
(paint when burned leaches into soil and lasts
up to forty-nine years)

And then, you planted.
Not like a refugee who seeds
only shallow roots
and dreams of return,

> but like Columbus, conquering: O, land . . .
> A vine of snap peas billowing lush on the chain-
> link fence
> hid us there in the center of the garden.
> Your sunflower

seven feet high, green sandpaper skin, like the mast of a ship rising tall

on the horizon.

It was time to take down the sail, last through felling
what was no longer useful.

We can give back: O,
collapse . . .

The choice a gardener makes, which neck to snap, and we are all
secondary, all but feeders on sunlight: O, forsaken child . . .

We must carry this useless body, head and foot, to the compost bin, toss it
in, give it back.

And the horizon was a house,

an old Victorian across the street, leaning far, threatening to fall
unless someone cleared the boards, painted a new exterior, hung
textiles in the windows, took an interest.

Exorcised the remains.

And the horizon was a dark river,

a street to the left sparkling in sunlight, broken glass
ground by tires turning glass into diamonds, or richer, fluid water
on black asphalt: O, vindication . . .

Nothing is the way it appears in explication, a ship sailing

in this ghetto,
tall yellow-petaled rag
fidgeting on its green mast

mildewed
in the last rain.

Your deck is full of other living: collards, kale, sweet basil,
all kinds of herbs, all kinds
of passion. I wish you could see,
you're no longer broken
or breaking,

　　　　what was once said is no longer real: O, never-resting mind . . .
　　　　the past is the past: O, petulant vine . . .
　　　　you can give back.

And abandon the dead surf of childhood: Say, beauty . . . Your beauty . . .
　　　　O, fine sword . . .

From their row of torn-out car seats on the sidewalk, we heard the
　　　　men (O, yes . . .) driving their conversation into argument and the
　　　　one in the middle looked up at us and rolled his eyes to heaven: O,
　　　　vibration . . .

　　　　Knife of horizon.

We began to saw back and forth
on the sunflower's seven-foot stalk, ant line
　　　　　　　　disintegrating
　　　　into soil, ants tickling our toes.

O, laughter . . . O, sister . . . To murder, one needs
only the simplest blade.

# NOTES

Several poems are based on or refer to photographs from Dorothea Lange's series *Death of a Valley*. I first came across a photograph from the series at an exhibit at the San Francisco MOMA, which sparked the writing of these poems. In the series, Lange documents the exodus from and destruction of California's fertile Berryessa Valley in preparation for creating the Berryessa Reservoir in 1957. I consulted a special 1960 issue of *Aperture*, with text by Pirkle Jones, during the writing of these poems.

The sources for the section epigraphs are: Ellen Bryant Voigt ("*Variations: At the Piano*"), Lewis Hyde (*The Gift*), John Steinbeck (*Travels with Charley*), Sigmund Freud (Letter to Lou Andreas-Salomé, May 25, 1916).

"Morphine": The line "whippy as a sheet . . . of stresses" is from *Gravity's Rainbow* by Thomas Pynchon.

"The Matter of the Pears": For the poet Kathy Garlick.

"Powerless Flight": After "Iris" by David St. John.

"Written Image": Based on an image in Maya Angelou's *I Know Why the Caged Bird Sings*.

"Okefenokee": The first line comes from a suggestion in *A Writer's Book of Days* by Judy Reeves.

"Mysticism in the Dark": The first five lines are adapted from a passage in *Things Fall Apart* by Chinua Achebe.

"Photograph: Antediluvians": The line "someone opens an orange in silence" is from Herberto Helder, translated from the Portuguese by Alexis Levitin. The ending is inspired by Czeslaw Milosz's poem "No More."

"Sunflower": After "Dead Doe" by Brigit Pegeen Kelly. The phrase "never-resting mind" is from "The Poems of Our Climate" by Wallace Stevens.